Published by

The Naval & Military Press Ltd
Unit 5 Riverside, Brambleside
Bellbrook Industrial Estate
Uckfield, East Sussex
TN22 1QQ England

Tel: +44 (0)1825 749494

www.naval-military-press.com
www.nmarchive.com

*In reprinting in facsimile from the original, any imperfections are inevitably reproduced
and the quality may fall short of modern type and cartographic standards.*

NOTES

ON

THE AREA

BETWEEN THE

River Somme, the St. Quentin and La Sensee Canals, and the River Scarpe.

Prepared by the General Staff

1916.

The Naval & Military Press Ltd

TABLE OF CONTENTS.

PART I.

	PAGE.
The area between the River Somme, the St. Quentin and La Sensee Canals, and the River Scarpe	5

GENERAL DESCRIPTION—

Geographical	5
Woods	5
Soil	5
Water	6
Villages	6
Meteorological	6
Industries	6
Population	6
Roads	7
Railways	7
Canals	7
Obstacles	7
System of defence	8

PART II.

The area between the River Somme, the St. Quentin Canal, and the Albert-Bapaume-Cambrai Railway	9
General	9
Towns and Villages	9
Rivers and Canals—	
Somme River—Somme Canal	10
Canal du Nord	10
St. Quentin Canal	12
Roads and Railways	12
Tactical	13

PART III.

The area between the Scarpe, the La Sensee Canal, and the Albert-Bapaume-Cambrai Railway	14
General	14
Soil	14

	PAGE
Water	14
Woods	14
Towns, etc.	14
Rivers and Canals—	
Upper Scarpe Canal	15
Sensee and Cojeul	15
Agache	15
Escaut	15
La Sensee Canal	16
Roads and Railways	16
Tactical	17
Defences	17

APPENDICES.

APPENDIX A.

Woods	19

APPENDIX B.

List of Towns and Villages	20

APPENDIX C.

List of Crossings over :	
River Scarpe (canalised)	28
Lr Sensee Canal	29
Le Cojeul River	29
La Sensee River	30
Escaut River (canalised))	32
St. Quentin Canal	32
St. Quentin and Crozat Canal	33
Somme River and Somme Canal	34
Germaine River	38
Omignon River	38
Cologne River	39
Tortille River	40
Canal du Nord	41

APPENDIX D.

List of Roads	43

APPENDIX E.

PAGE

Railway Bridges over :
    Scarpe River 44
    La Sensee Canal 44
    Le Cojeul River 44
    La Sensee River 45
    Escaut River (canalised) 45
    St. Quentin Canal... 45
    Somme Canal 46
    Tortille River 46
    Cologne River 46
    Omignon River 47
    Canal du Nord 47

PART I.

THE AREA BETWEEN THE RIVER SOMME, THE ST. QUENTIN AND LA SENSEE CANALS, AND THE RIVER SCARPE.

General description.

Geographical.—The area consists of a highly cultivated plateau intersected by the valleys of the tributaries of the SOMME and the ESCAUT. The main watershed is a well-defined ridge running West-North-West from BELLICOURT at a height of 470 to 550 ft. above sea level.

This plateau is undulating, and the main features run from South-West to North-East, falling steeply into the narrow valleys of the streams. The beds of the streams are usually marshy. The undulations provide numerous false crests.

The southern portion of the area is the highest, and thence the ground as a whole falls gently into the valleys of the SCARPE and LA SENSEE and into the plain of CAMBRAI. To the South the ground drops steeply into the valley of the SOMME and its tributary the COLOGNE, forming bluffs 80 to 100 ft. in height. The slopes are generally easy, the steepest being accessible to infantry. On the flanks of the spurs terraces with an abrupt drop of 3 to 15 ft. are a common feature. These do not constitute a serious obstacle, as they are not of great extent, and the flanks are always accessible.

The ground is generally open and unenclosed, except in the neighbourhood of the villages. On the whole, there is practically no restriction to the movement of the three arms from the accidents of the ground except in the valleys of the SOMME, the SCARPE and LA SENSEE.

The numerous indentations provide excellent cover except from aeroplanes, and the area is particularly well situated for the employment of cavalry, although the going in wet weather would be heavy.

Woods.—Woods and copses are numerous. The former are generally situated on the slopes of the spurs and extend from the bottom of the valley to the crest of the plateau. The undergrowth is usually thick and impenetrable, but this has probably been cut by the Germans.

Soil.—The subsoil is entirely composed of chalk covered on the plateau and gentle slopes by clay or stony deposits never very thick. The valleys are all more or less peaty below the surface. Turf pits, numerous cuts and ditches restrict movement at the bottom of the main valleys, which are fit for traffic when dry, but the ground cuts up rapidly after rain and the mud is bad. The soil, however, dries quickly.

Water.—Very little water is available on the plateau and slopes except that collected in cisterns or ponds. Plenty of water is available in the main valleys where streams exist for watering horses. Drinking water is obtained from wells and the water though incrusted is potable. On the plateau the wells may run to a depth of 300 ft. before the water level is reached. Between the SOMME and the OISE this level varies from 64 to 76 m., between the SOMME and the ESCAUT from 69 to 92 m., and North of the SOMME from 55 to 78 m. below the level of the ground.

In an advance the question of water supply will require special consideration, as the Germans will have destroyed all pumping machinery and may also have poisoned the wells.

Villages.—Owing to the absence of water on the plateau and slopes isolated farms are rare and the villages are mainly clustered in the valleys. The houses are fairly well and solidly built, but in the farms numerous barns and out-houses are built simply of lath and plaster.

Meteorological.—Thick fogs are common in the autumn, and prevailing winds are from the West, North-West and South-West, especially in the spring, and at the end of autumn.

Industries.—The staple industry is agriculture. West of the line, ARRAS—ALBERT, the cultivation is mostly of cereals. East of this line the sugar beet industry is all important. In the SOMME valley from ST. QUENTIN to HAM, and in the valleys of the COLOGNE, ESCAUT, SCARPE and SENSEE numerous sugar factories are situated.

In the cantons of ROISEL, COMBLES and BERTINCOURT many of the inhabitants, in addition to working on their farms, also weave and send their manufactures into ST. QUENTIN, which is the centre of the weaving industry. CAMBRAI, on the other hand, manufactures the extracts of the produce of the land such as chicory, beer, sugar, soap and the essential oils. It is also an important centre for bleaching the linen manufactured and brought in from the surrounding villages.

Population.—The density of the population varies according to the richness of the soil, and whether the inhabitants, in addition to cultivating the ground, are employed on manufactures. On poor soil the average density per square kilometre is 42 inhabitants, while in the neighbourhood of CAMBRAI the average rises to 199 inhabitants. In the cantons of MARQUION, BAPAUME and

BERTINCOURT, which may be considered as typical of the area, the average density is 100 inhabitants to the square kilometre.

Communications.

Roads.—The area is well intersected by good roads, every village being connected by a road practicable for the three arms under all conditions. The country roads, sometimes metalled, are only fit for traffic in dry weather.

The main roads are of three kinds, designated as under :—

Designation.	Average width of Metalling.	Average width between Ditches.
	Metres.	Metres.
1. Route Nationale	5	13
2. Chemins de Grande Communication	3½	7
3. Chemins Vicinaux Ordinaires	3	5½

Railways.—The area is well served by railways, the main trunk lines running to the North being doubled, while the cross lines linking up with the main AMIENS—ARRAS line are single. It is reported that the VELU—ST. QUENTIN line is being doubled.

Canals.—The Eastern boundary of the area is the Canal ST. QUENTIN, one of the main arteries for the carriage of coal from the North, and road metal, wood and grain to the North. To relieve the congestion of traffic, the Canal DU NORD from ARLEUX to PERONNE is under construction.

The network of waterways to the North and East is controlled by the enemy, who can turn the waters of the SCARPE into its old channel and so increase the marshes of the SENSEE, already a formidable obstacle. As the Germans will have not only mined but blocked the canals, their use for military purposes cannot be relied on until the obstructions are cleared.

Obstacles.—From the accidents of the ground, except the valleys of the SOMME, SCARPE and SENSEE, there are no obstacles to the movement of the three arms. The main obstacle is the unfinished Canal DU NORD which, starting at PERONNE, follows the valley of TORTILLE River to EQUANCOURT. Thence it is carried underground for over 4 km. to RUYAULCOURT, whence it runs *via* HAVRINCOURT and MARCOING to ARLEUX. The canal measures 11 ft. in depth and 65 to 80 ft. in width. Between HERMIES and HAVRINCOURT, it is carried through a cutting which reaches a depth of 34 m. in places.

Provision has been made for 34 bridges, but these will probably have been destroyed by the Germans.

There is a good deal of water in the Northern section, between HERMIES and HAVRINCOURT, and in the Southern between MOISLAINS and the SOMME.

Numerous cuttings on the VELU—ST. QUENTIN line between VELU and YTRES, and at VENDELLES, will restrict the movements of cavalry and guns.

On the PERONNE—CAMBRAI line, the main cuttings are in the neighbourhood of ROISEL, EPEHY and GOUZEAUCOURT.

System of defence.—The German system of defence is organised in two main lines. The first line is subdivided into three lines, the fire trench usually held as a line of observation, a supporting line about 100 m. behind the first trench, and a third or reserve line at varying distances in rear.

Behind the front line system are intermediate lines organised either (1) as retrenchments to salients, so as to form pockets or watertight compartments in order to localise any attack that may succeed in breaking through at any point, or (2) to defend high ground and thereby ensure observation, and so deny it to the enemy. These lines, though primarily defensive, being protected by wire, also offer facilities for massing troops for an offensive.

Behind the intermediate lines is the main second line of defence, at a distance of 3,000 to 5,000 yards behind the front line and sited on commanding ground. This line is at present largely a single line of traversed trench; but work has already started on a new support line in rear, and certain localities have been made into strong points.

Beyond these two lines, except for instructional works sited with a view to possible attacks, no other defensive works have been discovered.

East of ARRAS lines of entrenchments are reported by the French, and also on the right bank of the SENSEE stream.

As regards the organisation of the districts invaded by the Germans little is known. Kommandatur are at CAMBRAI and ST. QUENTIN.

Practically all the inhabitants of the villages situated within the first and main second German lines of defence, have been evacuated except at CURLU.

In rear of the German second line no general evacuation has been carried out.

PART II.

THE AREA BETWEEN THE RIVER SOMME, THE ST. QUENTIN CANAL, AND THE ALBERT—BAPAUME—CAMBRAI RAILWAY.

General.—The great bend in the River SOMME is due to the spur, running in a South-Westerly direction to HAM, which is thrown off from the main watershed at RANCOURT.

The area is intersected by the narrow valleys of the tributaries of the SOMME, and provides numerous positions, which form a barrier to any advance Eastwards. Two of these pivot on MT. ST. QUENTIN North of PERONNE, and the River SOMME adds to the difficulty by forming a natural obstacle to an advance South of the town. The main features have been described in Part I. and call for no further comment, but the difficulty of water supply is again emphasised. No water can be relied upon except in the valleys in which streams exist, and until the line of the CANAL DU NORD is mastered, drinking water will have to be sent up from the rear or from the SOMME.

The only wood of importance is that of HAVRINCOURT, but numerous others exist, the upper reaches of the TORTILLE stream being heavily wooded.

Towns and villages.—The most important town in the area is ST. QUENTIN, which lies on the North-West bank of the SOMME on ground sloping down to marshes. Low hills surround it in the form of a circle, which is broken by the valley of the SOMME running from South-West to North-East and by a ravine which separates the high ground to the North from that to the West

PERONNE is situated in a basin surrounded on all sides by high ground. The height of MT. ST. QUENTIN may be considered as the key of the place. For an attack from the West the occupation of the high ground by FLAUCOURT to the South-West, and the high ground to the North of CLERY would be the first objective, as from these heights an extensive view of the whole basin is obtained. The Germans have constructed a bridge across the marshes connecting the station of LA CHAPELLETTE with the town.

BAPAUME is the centre of numerous roads, and is visible from the high ground in the neighbourhood of MARTINPUICH. From

BAPAUME the ground slopes gently down to the plain of CAMBRAI. The buildings in the villages improve in quality in the neighbourhood of ST. QUENTIN owing to its being a brick-making centre.

Other villages call for no special comment except those in the valley of the COLOGNE in which numerous sugar factories are situated.

Rivers and canals.—Somme River and Somme Canal.—The SOMME from HAM to BETHENCOURT runs in a narrow constricted valley with steep banks. A canal runs alongside thus forming a double obstacle. The ground between the canal and river is often wooded and is subject to floods in winter.

Below BETHENCOURT the valley broadens out, and a water surface of from 200 to 600 yds. is fairly constant. This is caused by dykes and causeways which have been constructed across the valley at intervals, and which hold up the water above its natural level. The actual bed of the river is not visible, all that is seen is a series of lakes, some of which are very deep owing to excavations for turf.

The tributaries on either bank are all small, running in narrow marshy valleys, and are bridged at numerous places. They are shallow and offer no great obstacle to movement. A canal runs on the left bank of the river itself as far as BRAY and has a width of 55 ft. at water level and of 33 ft. at bottom. Depth of water is $6\frac{1}{2}$ ft. The slopes on either side of the valley vary, bluffs often 150 ft. on one side being faced by gentle slopes on the other.

A list of crossings of the river and canal, and the tributaries are given in Appendix C.

Canal du Nord.—Details of bridges are given in Appendix C.

Present state of the work

1. Completed—
    Origin to SAUCHY—CAUCHY (5·500 km.).
    INCHY en ARTOIS to Bridge No. 19 (12 km.).
    Between MANANCOURT and MOISLAINS (2·500 km.).

Water has been let into the Canal from the original to No. 1 Lock at PAILLEUL, a distance of about 1,500 m. The depth of water is $2\frac{1}{2}$ m. Between SAUCHY—CAUCHY and INCHY en ARTOIS the cuttings are muddy and wet. For 300 m. North of the underground portion and for 3,300 m. South of it, the cutting is filled with surface water, which attains a depth of 6 m. at the tunnel entrance.

Elsewhere the canal is empty.

Spoil banks have considerably modified the natural contour of the ground. The largest artificial mound reaches a height of 20 m. South of the BERTINCOURT—HERMIES Road.

2. Notes on cross sections of the canal—

  (a) In the deepest cuttings the walls of the canal are masonry, and above the tow-paths the banks are stepped, each step being 5 m. high.

  1. These deep cuttings exist at HAVRINCOURT, 900 m. North and 800 m. South of Bridge No. 16.
  2. Between Bridge No. 19 and the North end of the underground, except for about 150 m. South of Bridge No. 20 where the work is not far advanced.
  3. Between the Southern head of the underground and Bridge No. 22 about 800 m.

  (b) In the medium cuttings which occur for 120 m. above and below locks and in chalky soil, the canal walls are masonry, and the banks slant at 4/5. The canal could therefore only be crossed by infantry provided with ladders.

Cuttings of this type are found :—

  1. 250 m. North and South of Bridge No. 9.
  2. 500 m. South of Bridge No. 10.
  3. From 600 m. West of Bridge No. 12 to Bridge No. 16, except for 400 m. near Bridge No. 14.
  4. From 800 m. South of Bridge No. 16 to Bridge No. 19.
  5. Between Bridges Nos. 16 and 19.
  6. Between Bridges Nos. 30 and 31.
  7. For 300 m. South of Bridge No. 32.
  8. For 120 m. above and below completed locks all of which are above HAVRINCOURT.

  (c) Level crossings or points where the Canal offers no obstacle :—
    a. The RUYAULCOURT tunnel a length of 4,350 m.
    b. Where excavation has not yet been commenced.
    1. INCHY EN ARTOIS for a few hundred m. South of Bridge No. 8.
    2. MANANCOURT for 800 m. South of Bridge No. 25.
    3. For about 1 km. North of the CLERY—PERONNE Road.
    4. For about 200 m. South of the ALBERT—HAM railway.

3. Infantry can cross the SOMME Marshes between CLERY and PERONNE near BAZINCOURT Farm by the canal embankments,

which are connected with the North bank of the SOMME Canal by a foot-bridge.

An unmetalled towpath 4 to 6 m. wide runs along the whole length of the canal.

St. Quentin Canal.—This Canal joins the River SOMME to the River ESCAUT at CAMBRAI.

Between ST. SIMON and ST. QUENTIN it has a breadth of 60 ft. between banks, and 33 ft. at bottom. Between ST. QUENTIN and CAMBRAI, the breadth between banks is 66 ft., and of the bottom 40 ft.

The depth is $6\frac{1}{2}$ ft. to 7 ft. throughout. There are two lengths running underground, one about 1 km. long at LEHAUCOURT, the second $5\frac{1}{2}$ km. long between BELLICOURT and VENDHUILE.

There is a towpath on either bank varying from 9 to 23 ft. wide, metalled on the East bank only on a width of 8 to 14 ft.

Both banks are bordered by trees.

Bridges are fairly numerous and are usually of wood with masonry abutments.

A list of crossings is given in Appendix C.

Roads and railways.

Roads.—The area is well intersected by good roads, and as the Germans make little use of mechanical transport, these roads should be in good condition. The general trend of the roads is in a northerly direction, but cross roads are numerous. For a move Eastwards seven roads are available and are shown in colour on the map.

Railways.—The important bridges are those at PERONNE over the SOMME Canal, at HAVRINCOURT over the Canal DU NORD and at MARCOING over the ST. QUENTIN Canal.

Details of these bridges are shown in Appendix E.

The Germans have greatly extended the existing railways for the purposes of supply, and have linked up the railheads with light lines or trench tramways.

From PERONNE the existing metre gauge line has been extended from CLERY to BOUCHAVESNES, which is reported as the railhead of the 12th Division. As trains continue to run to COMBLES it appears that this new line has been constructed as a precautionary measure, owing to the proximity of the CLERY—COMBLES line to the front line trenches. If this be the case the line from PERONNE to BOUCHAVESNES has probably been made into normal gauge.

From BAPAUME a normal gauge line has been constructed along the main road as far as LE SARS (the railhead of the 28th Reserve Divison) whence a light line or trench tramway continues to MARTINPUICH, MAMETZ Wood and CONTALMAISON. This line may be continued to the East via CATERPILLAR Wood and the valley North of MONTAUBAN linking up with the existing metre gauge line at the BOIS DES TRONES.

Tactical.—The terrain is eminently suited for observation, large stretches of country being visible from any point on the plateau. False crests and the woods only restrict the view The numerous folds in the ground provide ample cover except from aeroplanes. The River ANCRE below MIRAUMONT forms a formidable obstacle having an unfordable marshy bottom from 300 to 400 m. in width.

The enemy's first line defences in this area are pivotted on the strongly defended localities of THIEPVAL, OVILLERS, LA BOISSELLE and FRICOURT. The salient of FRICOURT is well retrenched.

The main second line is sited on the higher ground from GRANDCOURT to GUILLEMONT, and thence to the SOMME.

The importance of the CONTALMAISON spur and the off-shoot to HARDECOURT from the spur running towards MAMETZ from GUILLEMONT has been fully recognised; intermediate lines to protect these points having been prepared, and forming bastions to the second line.

Work on the second line is not far advanced except East of POZIERES and from MAUREPAS to the SOMME.

Beyond these two lines, certain trenches have been dug in the neighbourhood of ROCQUIGNY, SAILLY, RANCOURT, BOUCHAVESNES and MONT ST. QUENTIN. These works appear to be instructional but are sited with a view to defence. No rear lines appear to exist, as repeated air reconnaissances have failed to discover them. Works of a defensive nature have been reported North-East of ST. QUENTIN.

PART III.

THE AREA BETWEEN THE SCARPE, THE LA SENSEE CANAL, AND THE ALBERT—BAPAUME—CAMBRAI RAILWAY.

General.—The characteristics of the ground in this area are similar to those in the Southern area, though the features are less marked. The ground as a whole slopes gently down from the South into the valleys of the SCARPE and LA SENSEE, and into the plain round CAMBRAI.

The general lie of the ground is a succession of long parallel spurs, thrown off from the main watershed, and running South West and North-East. These spurs are divided by the tributaries of the LA SENSEE, and finally merge into the marshes of the river and into the flats round CAMBRAI.

The main features are the high ground at MONCHY LE PREUX, a continuation of the VIMY ridge to the South of the SCARPE; and the marshes of the LA SENSEE and the AGACHE, which form an impassable obstacle and only crossed by few roads.

These marshes could be augmented by turning the water of the SCARPE down its old bed between BIACHES and VITRY, and by destroying the LA SENSEE Canal near the bend South of GOEULZIN.

Soil.—The subsoil is chalk with a covering, varying in thickness, of clay, which becomes very heavy after rain, but dries up quickly.

Water.—The same difficulties with regard to drinking water exist as in the Southern Sector, though the depth of the wells is not so great. Water for animals is always available in the lower reaches of the streams.

Woods.—Few woods exist, the only one of any size being that of BOURLON.

Towns, &c.—The most important town in the area is CAMBRAI, which is situated on undulating ground surrounded by a ring of low hills in the shape of an ellipse.

Encircling the town is a high wall with narrow exits.

The rest of the villages are small, and, owing to the difficulties of water, are situated in the valleys.

Rivers and Canals.

Upper Scarpe Canal.—Below ARRAS the River SCARPE IS CANALISED and joints the LA SENSEE at CORBEHEM.

From ARRAS to the junction it has a breadth of 45 ft. at water level and of 23 to 25 ft. at bottom. The depth of water is 6½ ft. There is a metalled towpath 20 ft. wide on the South bank.

Eight locks exist, one each at BLANGY, ATHIES, FAMPOUX, BIACHE, VITRY, and two at BREBIERES.

The approaches are marshy, especially on the South bank in the neighbourhood of ATHIES, FAMPOUX and BIACHES.

A list of crossings is given in Appendix C.

Sensee and Cojeul.—These two streams rise to the South of ARRAS and flow in a North-Easterly direction joining near ETERPIGNY, below which point the ground on either bank is marshy. They both form a somewhat serious obstacle to guns, being about 15 ft. wide with muddy bottoms.

Two deep narrow dykes, usually dry, also drain into the Cojeul and form a considerable obstacle to guns. One dyke starts at GOMMECOURT, passes the Northern edge of DOUCHY les AYETTE and joins the COJEUL near BOIRY ST. MARTIN. The second starts at BUCQUOY, passes AYETTE and joins the COJEUL between BOIRY BECQUERELLE and HENIN-sur-COJEUL.

At ETAING the marshes begin.

A list of crossings is given in Appendix C.

The Agache.—The valley of the AGACHE independently of the CANAL DU NORD, which also follows the valley, forms a serious obstacle owing to the marshes, which extend the whole way from INCHY EN ARTOIS to the junction with the LA SENSEE, except in the immediate neighbourhood of SAINS-LES-MARQUION.

A list of crossings is given in Appendix C.

The ESCAUT or SCHELDT is canalised from CAMBRAI.

The breadth of water level is 56 ft., and at bottom 33 ft., with a depth of water of 6 ft.

There is a towpath on either bank about 14 ft. broad metalled at intervals only.

The approaches away from the roads are not as a general rule good owing to irrigation ditches. The ground on the East bank about ESWARS is particularly marshy.

A list of crossings is given in Appendix C.

La Sensee Canal.—The average width at bottom is 33 ft., and at water level 66 to 70 ft. The depth of water is 8 ft., and the banks are 1 to 2 ft. above water.

The lock at FRESSIES and that South of GOEULZIN have been done away with, and this stretch has no lock between that situated on the West of GOEULZIN and the BASSIN ROND (junction of the LA SENSEE Canal and the ESCAUT Canal), a length of 28 km.

The canal has a weak point at the bend South of GOEULZIN where it would be easy to breach it. The volume of water which would inundate the country would be considerable, and would flood the valley from the bend in the canal to COURCELETTES for a width of at least 500 m. The two villages of GOEULZIN and FERRIN would be submerged.

The canal from GOEULZIN to FRESSIES has recently been deepened by 4 ft. It has consequently drained a quantity of water from the marshes, and also from the LA SENSEE stream between ARLEUX and FRESSIES.

The swamps to the North of HEMLENGLET, where the bridge is reported to have been destroyed by the Germans, have been partly filled in, but from FECHAIN to ESTRUN the marshy ground to the North of the canal is practically impassable except at the roads.

Between AUBIGNY AU BAC and FRESSIES, during dry weather, a passage should be practicable.

Between the bridge DES VACHES and the REDOUBT bridge at ARLEUX there is a basin for boats. The canal is on a level with the surrounding country as far as 1 km. North of ARLEUX Station, where there is a bridge which carries a Decauville light railway across the canal. From this point the canal runs through a deep cutting as far as the bridge of LE MOULINET, crossing the rising ground about ARLEUX, where the banks are from 12 to 25 ft. above the level of the water. From LE MOULINET onwards the canal is embanked, and a branch of the river at least 3 ft. below the level of the canal runs alongside it, as far as the lock West of GOEULZIN, where the depth of water in the river is 15 ft. There is a footbridge, difficult of access, at the bend of the canal to the North-East of the QUESNOY Wood. The bridges at FERRIN and BASSIN ROND are swing bridges.

A list of crossings is given in Appendix C.

Roads and Railways.

Roads.—Owing to the LA SENSEE Marshes, the roads leading Eastwards are restricted and are focussed into CAMBRAI, the apex of the triangle, of which the base is the line BAPAUME—ARRAS.

Only six good roads cross the marshes between LECLUSE and BOUCHAIN.

The crossings are: A small road in bad repair from LECLUSE to SAILLY, by the PONT DES VACHES. The road from LECLUSE to TORTEQUENNE is good and lined with houses the whole way.

Between LECLUSE and HAMEL is an indifferent footpath.

A good road leads from PALLUEL to ARLEUX, parallel to which is the CANAL DU NORD.

Further to the East is the LA SENSEE Canal, a good road from the ABBAYE DU VERGER farm to BRUNE MONT, the railway North of AUBENCHEUL AU BAC, the route Nationale No. 17 to AUBIGNY AU BAC, two indifferent crossings near HEMLENGLET, and good roads to WASNES AU BAC and BOUCHAIN.

The roads for a move Eastwards are coloured brown.

Details are given in Appendix D.

Railways.—The important bridges are those over the SCARPE at ARRAS, over the ST. QUENTIN Canal at CAMBRAI, and over the LA SENSEE Canal at AUBENCHEUL AU BAC.

Details are shown in Appendix E.

In this sector also the Germans have extended their railway system. From MIRAUMONT a line runs to PUISIEUX and thence to BUCQUOY. From ACHIET-LE-GRAND a line also runs to BUCQUOY past the BOIS DE LOGEAST, probably linking up with that from MIRAUMONT. As these lines both take off from a normal gauge line it is probable that the extension is normal gauge. An extension is also reported from the BOIS DE LOGEAST to ABLAINZEVILLE.

Tactical.—In the area the observation is good and possibly better than in the Southern sector, owing to the features being less marked. The terrain is well suited for movement by the three arms, except in the marshy area of the SENSEE.

Defences.—The enemy's front line of defence is pivotted on the villages of MONCHY, GOMMECOURT and BEAUMONT HAMEL, all of which form salients and are well retrenched.

SERRE and the high ground North of ESSARTS are also strongly defended.

The main second line is situated on the highest ground between ADINFER Wood and the ANCRE, and North of RANSART approaches more closely the front line system.

The system of defence North of RANSART does not appear to be well advanced, as the front line system only consists of two lines of trenches, and no intermediate lines exist; whereas between RANSART and the ANCRE serveral intermediate lines have been dug and wired.

The second line at present only consists of a single traversed trench, except North of BUCQUOY where the support line has been started.

East of ARRAS a line of entrenchments is reported by the French to exist on the line WANCOURT—MONCHY—LE PREUX—FAMPOUX and along the right bank of the SENSEE Stream from REMY to CHERISY.

CAMBRAI, as far as can be ascertained, has not been fortified.

APPENDIX A.

WOODS.

The trees in the woods are mostly beech, oak, ash and birch surrounded by a thick undergrowth of brambles, thorns, maples and willows, which, if five or six years old, make an impenetrable screen. This undergrowth has probably been cut and removed by the Germans for use in the trenches, or as firewood, so the woods would probably offer no obstacles to the movements of infantry.

Probably also a great deal of the timber has been cut down and removed. A saw mill is located at the BOIS DE LOGEAST.

No data are forthcoming as to the woods of HAVRINCOURT, BOURLON and those on the banks of the TORTILLE Stream.

APPENDIX B.

Village.	No. of houses.	No. of inhabitants.	Wells.	Ponds.	Remarks.
Abancourt	148	610	115	—	Chateau.
Achiet-le-Grand	133	528	38	2	
Aizecourt, Le Bas	88	341	8	5	1 weaving factory.
Aizecourt, Le Haut	58	144	8	5	
Allaines	318	642	60	40	
Arleux	411	1,688	42	1	Sugar factory, glass factory.
Athies (Arras)	113	505	90	1	Oil mill, brewery, foundry, repair shops.
Athies (Ham)	300	1,157	120	—	Sugar factory.
Aubencheul-au-Bac	119	476	82	1	Sugar factory
Aubigny-au-Bac	223	977	52	1	
Avesnes-les-Bapaume	75	235	18	1	1 cloth factory, brick kiln.
Ayette	100	479	30	—	
Bantigny	106	512	80	—	2 sugar factories.
Bapaume	735	3,144	37	2	Sugar factory, oil factory.
Barastre	180	687	90	—	Oil factory.
Beaulencourt	103	454	36	2	
Beaumetz-les-Cambrai	330	1,269	111	2	Brick kiln, brewery.
Beaurains	230	1,092	88	10	Brewery.
Beauvois	191	602	30	—	School.
Behagnies	58	235	26	—	Steam saw-mills.
Bellenglise	188	774	83	7	Saw yard, cloth factory.
Bellonne	53	172	18	—	
Bernes	188	598	13	5	Sugar factory.
Bethencourt	57	196	30	—	
Beugnatre	60	188	25	9	Farm Delsaux, Farm Raperie.
Beugny	168	671	80	5	Brick kiln, sugar factory, metal works.
Biache-St. Vaast	337	2,073	120	—	
Biefvillers-les-Bapaume	42	179	14	2	

Bihucourt	...	94	344	28	7	
Blecourt	...	82	407	2	2	
Boiry-Becquerelle	...	80	303	10	2	
Boiry-Notre Dame	...	161	623	100	—	
Boisleux-au-Mont	...	110	461	37	1	Sugar factory.
Boisleux-St. Marc	...	56	175	18	—	
Bony	...	119	361	4	1	Cloth factory.
Bouchavesnes	...	202	552	42	12	Factory.
Bourlon	...	378	1,950	54	—	
Boursies	...	179	808	35	5	Sugar factory, brewery, distillery.
Boyelles	...	87	357	6	—	
Bray-St. Christophe		61	158	40	3	
Brebieres	...	414	1,837	148	25	2 sugar factories.
Brie	...	151	467	50	25	Sugar factory.
Bullecourt	...	125	506	30	2	Sugar factory.
Buire	...	151	467	50	25	Sugar factory.
Bus	...	81	252	14	2	
Buseu	...	158	389	50	20	
Cagnicourt	...	241	825	81	—	2 breweries.
Cambrai	...	—	28,077	—	—	Numerous factories.
Cantaing	...	152	672	90	2	Chateau.
Cartigny	...	266	1,609	105	3	Sugar factory.
Caulaincourt	...	108	365	78	2	Chateau.
Cherisy	...	146	527	30	1	Sugar factory, brewery.
Clery	...	238	976	48	19	1 foundry.
Combles	...	458	1,440	38	4	Lepiez Farm, 1 sugar Factory, 7 spinning and weaving factories.
Contescourt	...	48	178	14	2	Sugar factory.
Courcelette	...	99	309	19	—	1 sugar factory, foundry.
Courcelles-le-Comte	...	195	739	10	—	
Croisilles	...	340	1,555	60	1	Sugar factory, brewery.
Croix-Molignaux	...	147	409	14	2	
Cuvillers	...	72	370	53	2	
Doignies	...	183	798	30	4	Sugar factory, chateau.
Douilly	...	122	582	111	2	Sugar factory, distillery.
Driencourt	...	111	303	26	16	

APPENDIX B—continued.

Village.	No. of houses.	No. of inhabitants.	Wells.	Ponds.	Remarks.
Dury (St. Simon)	180	392	60	12	
Dury (Vitry)	113	451	104	—	
Ecourt-St. Quentin	569	1,859	281	—	Sugar factory, brewery.
Ecoust-St. Mein	147	731	27	2	Sugar factory.
Ennemain	102	354	85	2	Brewery.
Epehy	400	1,685	32	4	Brewery, 6 spinning factories.
Epinoy	189	750	30	—	Rope factory, sugar factory.
Equencourt	209	808	64	9	2 breweries, 1 spinning factory.
Ervillers	192	827	25	1	
Estrees	235	1,024	80	1	
Eswars	117	479	100	—	Chateau.
Etaing	164	608	27	—	
Eterpigny	60	247	52	—	
Etreillers	329	1,101	60	8	Disused workhouse.
Etrun	119	642	100	—	
Falvy	131	328	64	3	
Fampoux	253	1,015	45	—	Oil factory, sugar factory, brewery.
Favreuil	93	312	28	12	Cloth factory.
Fayet	209	427	19	—	Chateau.
Ferin	160	800	26	1	Flax mill, brewery, sugar factory.
Feuchy	116	523	60	1	Foundry, repair shops, cardboard factory.
Fins	134	563	12	6	Sugar factory.
Flers	164	577	14	—	
Floquieres	170	764	90	10	Sugar factory, weaving mill.
Fontaine-les-Croisilles	127	461	14	—	
Fontaine-Notre Dame	437	1,967	112	2	
Fremicourt	100	427	45	6	
Fressies	158	687	110	1	

23

Germaine	53	195	35	Cheese factory.
Ginchy	64	199	7	
Gomiecourt	50	225	—	
Gouy-sous-Bellonne	181	791	97	Sugar factory.
Grevillers	163	606	47	School.
Gricourt	190	774	88	Factory.
Guemappe	109	398	90	Sugar factory.
Gueudecourt	95	299	24	
Guillemont	157	414	10	
Guyencourt-Saulcourt	162	510	13	
Ham	570	3,254	400	Numerous factories, fortress, barracks.
Hamblain-les-Pres	106	472	80	
Hamel	116	422	95	
Hamelincourt	122	425	40	
Hancourt	68	221	12	
Haplincourt	125	523	34	
Happencourt	135	412	10	
Hardecourt-au-Bois	137	509	10	Phosphate factory, knacker's yard.
Hargicourt	275	1,475	25	Sugar factory, detached farm.
Havrincourt	248	1,094	114	Sugar factory, 3 breweries.
Hem-Lenglet	184	751	130	
Hendecourt-les-Cagnicourt	168	589	65	
Heninel	55	260	25	
Hermies	582	2,530	65	Sugar factory.
Hervilly	119	356	40	2 cloth factories.
Hesbecourt	70	227	8	3 cloth factories, sugar factory, brewery.
Heudicourt	315	1,362	60	Brewery.
Holnon	207	655	74	Sugar factory.
Hombleux	316	1,021	300	
Inchy-en-Artois	260	1,037	194	2 alcohol factories, several breweries.
Iwuy	820	3,890	300	Distillery, sugar factory.
Jeancourt	200	600	34	Poor area.
Lagnicourt	153	572	99	Brewery.

24

APPENDIX B—continued.

Village.	No. of houses.	No. of inhabitants.	Wells.	Ponds.	Remarks.
Languevoisin	88	264	42	—	Brewery.
Le Catelet	122	545	46	—	Farm des Quatre Vents.
Lechelle	50	119	5	—	2 sugar factories, 2 breweries.
Lecluse	413	1,790	305	4	
Leforest	27	78	38	6	Cloth factory.
Le Mesnil-en-Arrouaise	118	377	13	3	1 farm, poor area.
Lempire	126	489	6	3	1 factory, 1 sugar factory.
Le Sars	172	512	36	7	
Lesbœufs	169	432	20	3	Steam mill, sugar factory, brick kiln.
Le Transloy	413	1,320	85	2	
Le Verguier	188	532	10	12	1 sugar factory, 1 factory.
Lieramont	200	701	16	10	Steam mill.
Ligny-Thilloy	219	755	94	4	1 factory.
Longavesnes	70	227	7	—	Sugar factory.
Longueval	130	406	8	17	
Malsseny	153	502	74	9	2 sugar factories, 1 cloth factory.
Manancourt	369	1,179	80	3	Cloth factory.
Marche-le-Pot	156	454	100	15	Several factories.
Marqualx	96	392	64	—	2 sugar factories, 1 hat factory.
Marquion	181	825	136	4	
Matigny	228	930	200	—	2 farms, brewery.
Maurepas	196	507	8	3	
Metz-en-Couture	365	1,580	54	2	
Misery	83	305	61	4	3 factories.
Mœuvres	208	858	90	—	Sugar factory.
Moislains	252	1,477	40	1	Brewery, brick kiln.
Monchy-Lagache	258	1,089	140	—	Sugar factory.
Monchy-le-Preux	172	726	80	5	
Mons-en-Chaussee	210	679	79		

Montauban	...	274	511	6	7	Sugar factory.
Mont-St. Quentin	...	62	254	29	3	Sugar factory, machine shop.
Morchain	...	120	356	—	—	Brewery.
Morchies	...	118	503	30	2	
Morval	...	98	245	19	2	Brewery.
Mory	...	151	600	45	—	
Moyenneville	...	92	380	37	—	
Nesle	...	584	2,285	34	3	Sugar factory, distillery, brewery.
Neuville-St. Remy	...	182	1,125	129	1	Several factories.
Neuville-Vitasse	...	157	608	75	—	Sugar factory.
Noreuil	...	106	296	32	—	Distillery.
Noyelles	...	143	710	100	3	Sugar factory.
Noyelle-St. Bellonne	...	141	546	51	—	
Nurlu	...	182	858	12	20	2 mills.
Offoy	...	99	393	74	3	
Oisy-le-Verger	...	468	2,197	110	—	Several factories.
Omiecourt	...	80	228	50	1	
Paillencourt	...	209	1,227	120	5	Brewery.
Pargny	...	80	238	70	5	3 printing works, numerous factories of all kinds, barracks.
Peronne	...	1,013	4,816	100	2	
Pithon	...	83	110	17	4	
Pœuilly	...	87	234	24	—	1 sugar factory.
Pontru	...	139	644	30	—	Sugar factory, chemical works.
Pontruet	...	105	463	90	6	Brewery.
Pronville	...	161	687	53	—	Stone quarry.
Proville	...	60	737	120	—	
Punchy	...	51	138	50	1	
Puzeaux	...	52	167	26	3	
Queant	...	264	980	92	—	Sugar factory, distillery, 2 breweries.
Quivieres	...	121	380	102	—	Sugar factory.
Ramillies	...	116	518	80	—	
Rancourt	...	99	309	9	12	Cloth factory.

APPENDIX B—continued.

Village.	No. of houses.	No. of inhabitants.	Wells.	Ponds.	Remarks.
Recourt	50	145	12	—	
Remy	83	296	50	—	
Rethouvillers	117	418	80	3	
Riencourt-les-Bapaume	23	77	8	1	
Riencourt-les-Cagnicourt	150	520	25	—	
Rœux	143	1,012	80	—	Sugar factory, brewery.
Roisel	395	1,758	160	20	1 brewery, 8 factories, Farm Nobecourt.
Ronssoy	319	1,385	16	18	7 factories.
Roupy	131	466	90	3	Sugar factory, spinning mill, brewery.
Sailly	125	592	62	1	
Sailly-Saillisel	256	812	20	12	2 factories.
Sains-los-Marquion	130	451	61	—	Breweries.
St. Christ Briost	145	527	50	2	
St. Leger	171	784	50	—	Sugar factory.
St. Quentin	5,577	47,551	5,000	—	Numerous factories, barracks for regiment.
St. Simon	158	613	113	11	Sugar factory, brewery.
Senconrt	125	389	113	2	
Sapignies	80	267	39	7	
Saranconrt-le-Grand	364	1,376	87	4	3 factories.
Sauchy-Cauchy	155	568	145	—	Tile factory, brewery, brick kiln.
Sauchy-Lestree	191	723	145	—	Tile factory.
Saudemont	173	536	104	—	2 breweries.
Savy	198	614	93	3	Brick kiln.
Sorel	256	812	15	1	1 factory.
Templeux-la-Fosse	184	699	12	15	3 phosphate factories.[1]
Tertry	101	368	80	1	
Tilloy	62	365	20	1	Chateau.

27

Tilloy-les-Mofflaines	...	119	483	25	2	
Tincourt-Boucly	...	172	735	100	1	
Tortequenne	...	149	537	65		
Tugny et Pont	...	167	614	79	6	Brewery, factory.
Vaulx Vraucourt	...	372	1,550	72		Numerous factories.
Vaux	...	59	178	45	4	Chateau.
Vendelles	...	77	326	14	3	Detached farms.
Vendhuille	...	377	1,681	100		3 detached farms, sugar factory, brick works, factory.
Vermand	...	372	1,247	104	10	Brick works, 2 factories.
Villeret	...	146	930	3		1 detached farm, poor area.
Villers-au-Flos	...	197	592	75	2	
Villers-Faucon	...	341	1,392	50		1 sugar factory, 1 factory.
Villers-les-Cagnicourt	...	88	324	46		Sugar factory.
Villers St. Christophe	...	241	817	200	8	Sugar factory.
Vis-en-Artois	...	153	766	116		Sugar factory, tile factory.
Vitry-en-Artois	...	673	2,910	304		Numerous factories.
Voyennes	...	240	814	60	2	
Vraignes	...	78	253	17	8	1 brewery, 1 factory.
Wancourt	...	144	572	60		
Warlencourt	...	56	188	36	1	2 breweries.
Ytres	...	242	886	66	2	Factory.

APPENDIX C.

BRIDGES OVER THE RIVER SCARPE (CANALISED).

Town.	Identification on squared map, 1/40,000.	Length, metres.	Breadth, metres.	Type.		Remarks.
Arras	Sheet 51. B. G. 16d. ...	—	4·50	Girder ...	Masonry abutments	Private road.
,, (Lock) ...	Sheet 51. B. G. 16c. ...	38·50	5·20	—	Masonry	Quatre-Crics or St. Nicolas Lock.
St. Laurent ...	Sheet 51. B. G. 18. 24 ...	5·20	8·	Girder ...	...	Douai—Arras Road (Route Nle.).
,, (Lock)	Sheet 51. B. G. 17. 23 ...	38·50	5·20	—	Masonry	Blangy Lock.
Athies (Lock) ...	Sheet 51. B. H. 21a. ...	38·50	5·20	—	,,	Chin. de Gde. Comm. No. 37.
,, ...	Sheet 51. B. H. 21a. ...	6·60	4·30	Girder ...	Skew shaped ...	Chin. de Gde. Comm. No. 37.
Fampoux (Lock)	Sheet 51. B. H. 17. 23 ...	38·60	5·20	—	Masonry	Fampoux - Monchy Road (Chemin vicinal).
,, ...	Sheet 51. B.H. 17. 23 ...	5·20	4·34	Girder ...	Roadway 2·70	Fampoux - Monchy Road (Chemin vicinal).
Roeux	Sheet 51. B. I. 19d ...	9·72	4·30	,, ...	Masonry abutments	Henin-Estaires Road (Ch. de Gde. Comm.).
Biache (Lock) ...	Sheet 51. B. I. 17b. ...	38·75	—	—	Masonry	Ch. de Gde. Comm. No. 42.
,, ...	Sheet 51. B. I. 17b. ...	...	3·60	Girder (drawbridge)	—	,,
Vitry	Sheet 51. B. J. 2a	10·	4·10	Girder...	Masonry abutments, paved roadway	Saudemont-Vernelles Road (Ch. de Gde,Comm.)
Brebieres (Lock)	Sheet 51. B. D. 23c.d.	38·20	5·20	—	Masonry	Ch. de Gde. Comm. No. 44.
Corbehem (Lock)	Sheet 51. B. E. 19d.	38·68	5·20	—	,,	Corbehem Lock.
,, ,,	Sheet 51. B. E. 19d.	—	3·70	Girder (swing-bridge)	Masonry abutments	Hermitage-Corbehem Road (Ch.de Gde,Comm.).
,, ,,	Sheet 51. B. E. 19b.d.	27·	2·	Girder (foot-bridge)	Masonry abutments	

BRIDGES OVER LA SENSEE CANAL.

Courchelettes	(51B.) E. 14b.	5·20	4·	Wood	Masonry abutments	Couchelettes — Lambres Road (Ch. vicinal).
Ferin	(51B.) K. 3a, c.	8·	4·20	"	Masonry abutments	Douai — Bapaume Road (Ch. de Gde. Comm.).
Cantin	(51B.) K. 17a.	6·	3·80	"	Masonry abutments	Goeulzin—Arleux Road.
Arleux	(51B.) L. 31a.	8·	3·70	Girder	Masonry abutments	Arleux—Orchies Road (Ch. de Gde. Comm.).
"	—	7·	3·16	"	Masonry abutments	Mouth of La Sensee River.
Oisy	(51B.) R. 8d.	5·50	4·	Wood	Masonry abutments	Oisy—Bugnicourt Road.
Aubigny-au-Bac	(51B.) R. 16a.	5·41	3·10	Drawbridge (iron)	Timber roadway	Paris—Lille Road (Route Nle).
Fressies (Lock)	51 A	5·20	3·10	Drawbridge (iron)	—	Fressies Lock.
Hem-Lenglet	51 A	6·	3·70	Girder	Masonry abutments	Marquette—Neuville Road (Ch. de Gde. Comm.), (said to have been destroyed by the Germans).
Paillencourt	51 A	5·90	—	Wood	Masonry abutments	
Etrun	51 A	6·	4·	"	Masonry abutments	Private road.
Hordain (Lock)	51 A	5·20	—		Masonry	Bassin—Nord.

BRIDGES OVER LE COJEUL RIVER.

Boiry St. Rictrude	(51B.) S. 19d.	8·20	7·30	—	Masonry	Mailly—Arras Road (Ch. de Gde. Comm.).
"	(51B.) S. 14d.	8·90	8·30	—	"	Achiet—Boiry Road (Ch. de Gde. Comm.).
Bolsleux-au-Mont	(51B.) S. 10c.	5·90	6·50	2 arches	"	Lagnicourt—Ficheux Road (Ch. de Gde. Comm.).
"	(51B.) S. 11c.	8·	3·50	—	"	Monchy—Henin Road (Ch. de Gde. Comm.).

APPENDIX C—continued.

Town.	Identification on squared map, 1/40,000.	Length, metres.	Breadth, metres.	Type.	Remarks.
BRIDGES OVER LE COJEUL RIVER—continued.					
Boiry-Becquerelle	(51b.) S. 12b.	14·	13·	—	Masonry	Chateau Thierry—Bethune Road (Route Nle.).
Henin-Sur Cojeul	(51b.) T. 7a.	8·10	3·	—	,,	Monchy — Henin Road (Ch. de. Gde. Comm.).
" "	(51b.) T. 2b.	5·34	5·00	—	,,	Arras—Havrincourt Road.
St. Martin-sur-Cojeul	(51b.) N. 33a.	12·70	1·35	—	,,	St. Martin—Groisilles Road (Ch. vicinal).
" "	(51b.) N. 33a.	6·15	2·50	—	,,	St. Martin—Fontaine Road (Ch. vicinal).
Heninel	(51b.) N. 28d.	·70	2·10	—	,,	Heninel — Cherisy Road (Ch. vicinal).
Wancourt	(51d.) N. 23b.	5·60	4·45	—	,,	Wancourt—Cherisy Road (Ch. vicinal).
Guemappe	(51b.) N. 24b.	5·10	3·35	—	,,	Queant—Arras Road (Ch. de Gde. Comm.).
Vis-en-Artois	(51b.) O. 13, 14	5·	3·	—	,,	Country road.
"	(51b.) O.15d.	8·40	6·80	3 arches	,,	Montreuil—Mezieres Road (Route Nle.).
Remy	(51b.) O. 11c.	4·54	—	—	,,	Miraumont—Etaing Road (Ch. de. Gde. Comm.).
" "	—	3·	2·50	Wood	Masonry, wooden abutments.	Road to mill.
BRIDGES OVER LA SENSEE RIVER.					
Ervillers	(57c.) B. 7	15·	4·40	...	Masonry	Chateau Thierry—Bethune Road (Route Nle.).

St. Leg	...	(51b.) T. 28c.	...	7·95	4·90	...	,,	Ch. de Gde. Comm. No. 36.
,,	...	(51b.) T. 28d.	...	4·50	3·	...	,,	Road leading to St. Leger Wood.
Croisilles	...	(51b.) T. 23d.	...	6·	2·	...	,,	Ch. de Gde. Comm. No. 9.
,,	...	(51b.) T. 24a.	...	7·90	5·	...	,,	Havrincourt—Arras Road (Ch. de Gde. Comm.).
Fontaine-les Croisilles	(51b.) U. 2b.	...	8·	3·	...	,,	Miraumont—Etaing Road (Ch. de Gde. Comm.).
Cherisy	...	(51b.) O. 32b.	...	8·	3·30	...	,,	Queant—Arras Road (Ch. de Gde. Comm.).
Vis-en-Artois	...	(51b.) O. 23c.	...	4·	6·50	...	Masonry, paved roadway.	Montreuil—Mezierres Road (Route Nle.).
Remy	...	(51b.) O. 18c.	...	4·	4·80	...	Masonry	Miraumont—Etaing Road (Ch. de Gde. Comm.).
Eterpigny & Etaing	—		4·20	4·	...	Masonry, wooden abutments, paved roadway.	Saudemont — Vermelles Road (Ch. de Gde. Comm.).
,,	,,	(51b.) P. 3a.	...	4·	4·50	Wood ...	Masonry abutments.	Etaing—Sailly Road.

31

APPENDIX C—continued.

Town.	Length, Metres.	Breadth, Metres.	Type.	Remarks.

BRIDGES OVER THE RIVER ESCAUT (CANALISED).

Town.	Length, Metres.	Breadth, Metres.	Type.	Remarks.
Cambrai	12·	—	Wood	Masonry abutments (2 roadways, 2·50 each). Route Nationale No. 29.
,,	15·	3·60	Swingbridge (iron)	Masonry abutments. ,, ,, No. 17.
,,	9·75	4·30	Girder	Masonry abutments (paved roadway). Country road.
Escaudœuvres	9·	4·50	,,	Masonry abutments. ,, ,,

BRIDGES OVER THE ST. QUENTIN CANAL.

Town.	Length, Metres.	Breadth, Metres.	Type.	Remarks.
Honnecourt (Lock)	34·65	5·18	—	Masonry ... Bosquet Lock.
,,	34·81	5·20	—	,, ... Moulin Lafosse Lock.
,,	34·65	5·20	—	,, ... Honnecourt Lock.
Banteux	34·75	5·35	—	,, ... Banteux Lock.
Bantouzelles	34·68	5·45	—	,, ... Bantouzelles Lock.
,,	—	9·	—	Route Nle. No. 44.
Crevecœur (Lock)	34·72	5·20	—	Masonry ... Vaucelles Lock.
,,	34·73	5·22	—	,, ... Tordoir Lock.
,,	34·67	5·20	—	,, ... Vinchy Lock.
,,	34·71	5·28	Arch...	,, ... Crevecœur Lock.
,,	34·65	5·34	—	,, ... St. Waast Lock.
Masnieres	34·64	5·20	—	,, ... Masnieres Lock.
,,	—	8·	—	Route Nle., No. 47.
,, (Lock)	34·64	5·17	—	,, ... Bracheux Lock.
Marcoing ,,	34·67	4·60	Girder	Masonry abutments. Marcoing Lock.

33

Noyelles	...	34·69	5·22	Girder	Masonry	Talma Lock.
"	...	—	5·	—	"	Ch. de Gde. Comm. No. 63.
" (Lock)	...	34·74	5·15	3 arches (5 metres each)	"	Noyelles Lock.
Proville	...	34·64	—	Girder	"	Cantigneul Lock.
"	...	34·68	5·20	—	"	Proville Lock.
Vendhuile	...	9·30	7·87	Girder	—	Roisel—Vendhuile Road (Ch. de Gde Comm.).
Bellicourt	...	8·	4·98	—	Masonry	Bellicourt—Riqueval Road (Ch. vicinal ordinaire).
Bellenglise	...	9·	5·	Girder	Roadway 3	Vermand to Chateau (Ch. de Gde. Comm.).
"	...	11·8	7·60	—	Masonry	Chalons—Cambrai Road (Route Nle.).
Le Haucourt	...	8·	5·15	—	"	Chemin vicinal ordinaire.
Lesdins (Lock No. 2)	...	5·20	—	—	Roadway 4·20	St. Quentin—Le Cateau Road (Ch. de Gde. Conm.).
Omissy (Lock No. 3)	...	5·20	5·—	—	" 2·60	Morcourt—Omissy Road (Ch. vicinal ordinaire).
Rouvroy (Lock No. 4)	...	5·20	—	—	" 2·60	St. Quentin—Guise Road.
St. Quentin	...	8·05	—	Girder	" 2·60	St. Quentin—Rouvroy Road (Ch. vicinal ordinaire).
"	...	5·50	—	—	" 7·95	Rouen—La Capelle Road (Route Nle.).

BRIDGES OVER THE ST. QUENTIN AND CROZAT CANALS.

Oestres	...	6·72	3·0	Wood	—	Private road.
Fontaine-les-Clercs (Lock No. 6)	...	7·50	—	"	Roadway 2·40	Fontaine — Castres Road (Chemin vicinal).
Seraucourt	...	6·70	2·90	"	—	Flavy-le-Martel—RoupyRoad (Ch. de Gde. Comm.).
Artemps	...	8·60	2·38	Swingbridge(metal)	—	Leading to mill.
Tugny (Lock No. 8)	...	—	6·26	Wood	Roadway 3·0	Caulaincourt — St. Simon Road (Ch. de Gde. Comm.).
St. Simon	...	9·05	—	Girder	" 2·60	Flavy-le-Martel—RoupyRoad (Ch. de Gde. Comm.).

APPENDIX C—*continued.*

BRIDGES OVER SOMME RIVER AND SOMME CANAL.

Town.	Length, metres.	Breadth, metres.	Type.		Remarks.
Morcourt	3·50	5·	Arch	Masonry	Morcourt—Omissy Road (Ch. vicinal).
"	3·20	11·50	"	"	St. Quentin—Gulse Road.
Rouvroy	3·75	8·25	"	"	Rouvroy—St. Quentin Road (Ch. vicinal).
St. Quentin	5·70	10·	Girder	Roadway 7	Rouen—La Capelle Road (Route Nle).
"	10·	2·60	"	—	St. Quentin—Rouvroy Road (Ch. vicinal).
"	5·	3·	"	Masonry abutments, roadway 2·50	Private road, Digue de Rocourt to Gauchy.
"	8·	2·60	"	Masonry abutments, roadway 2·20 and pier	Private road, Digue de Rocourt to Gauchy (over 2nd Mill race).
"	4·50	3·	"	Masonry abutments, roadway 2.	Private road, Digue de Rocourt to Gauchy (over 1st Mill race).
Gauchy	12·	4·50	"	Masonry abutments, roadway 3.	Gauchy—Oestres Road (Ch. vicinal).
Fontaine-les-Clercs	8·40	4·	4 arches	Masonry, roadway 3.	Fontaine—Castre Road (Ch. vicinal).
Seraucourt-le-Grand	8·20	4·50	4 "	Masonry, roadway 3.	Flavy-le-Martel—Roupy Road (Ch. de Gde. Comm.).
Happencourt	2·	4·50	Culvert (wood)	Roadway 3	Happencourt—Artemps Road (Ch. vicinal).
"	5·	4·50	Wood	" 3	Happencourt—Artemps Road (Ch. vicinal).

35

Location			Type	Details	Road
Artemps	...	9·	Girder	2 spans	Artemps—Happencourt Road (Ch. vicinal).
,,	...	5·50	Wood	Roadway 3	Artomps—Happencourt Road (Ch. vicinal).
Tugny and Pont	...	9·95	Girder	Roadway, 4·50	Caulaincourt—St. Simon Road (Ch. de Gde. Comm.).
Dury	...	9·0		Masonry, roadway 3·0.	Dury—Ollezy Road (Ch. vicinal).
Pithon	...	10·80	Wood (3 arches)	Masonry abutments.	Road leading to mill and marshes.
,,	...	4·80	Wood	Masonry abutments.	Road leading to mill and marshes.
Estouilly	...	12·0	Wood (timber pier)	Masonry abutments.	Estouilly Road.
Ham	...	5·70	Arch (span 4·70)	Masonry	Rouen — La Capelle Road (Route Nle.).
,,	...	5·90	2 arches (span 1·92 each).	Masonry	Under mill race.
Ham (No. 2 Lock) (upper) over canal	...	6·50	Girder		Chateau—Thierry—Bethune Road (Route Nle).
Ham (No. 3 Lock) (lower) over canal	...	6·45	,,		Rouen—La Capelle Road (Route Nle).
Offoy	...	8·50	Wood (2 spans)		Matigny—Libermont Road (Ch. de Gde. Comm.).
,,	...	6·40	Wood (iron girders)	Masonry abutments.	Matigny—Libermont Road (Ch. de Gde. Comm.).
,, over canal	...	6·75	Girder		Matigny—Libermont Road (Ch. de Gde. Comm.).
Voyennes	...	11·50	Wood (2 spans)		Languevoison—Vaux Road (Ch. de Moyenne Comm.).
,, over canal	...	8·68	Girder	Masonry abutments.	Languevoison—Vaux Road (Ch. de Moyenne Comm.).
Bethencourt	...	9·20	Wood	Masonry abutments, piers (2).	Nesle—Roisel Road (Ch. de Gde. Comm.).
,,	...	8·75	,,	Masonry abutments, piers (2).	Nesle—Roisel Road (Ch. de Gde. Comm.).
,, over Canal	...	14·68	Swingbridge (iron girders)	Distance between abutments 6·65.	Nesle—Roisel Road (Ch. de Gde. Comm.).

APPENDIX C—*continued.*

BRIDGES OVER SOMME RIVER AND SOMME CANAL—*continued.*

Town.	Length, metres.	Breadth, metres.	Type.		Remarks.
Pargny	8·95	3·68	Girder	Masonry abutments.	Ennemain—Nesle Road (Ch. de Moyenne Comm.).
Falvy	10	3·70	Wood (2 span)	Masonry abutments and pier.	Road No. 103, from Ennemain to Nesle.
,,	4½	3·70	Arch (1 span)	Masonry	Over mill race.
,,	4·40	3·88	Wood (1 span)	Masonry abutments.	
Epenancourt	15½	3·80	,, (7 ,,)	Masonry abutments, piles.	Road from Pertain to Falvy, over mill race.
,,	7·80	3·30	,, (2 ,,)	Masonry abutments wooden	Lock underneath Bridge to Falvy.
Lock No. 5 over canal	6½	3·70	Girder (1 span)	Masonry abutments and pier.	Road from Pertain.
St. Christ	7	6	,, (1 ,,)		Road No. 45, from Chaulnes to Vermand.
,,	7	6	,,	Masonry abutments.	Road No. 45, from Chaulnes to Vermand.
,,	3	6	,,	Masonry abutments.	Road No. 45, from Chaulnes to Vermand.
Over canal	8·70	5·25	,, (1 span)	Masonry abutments.	Road No. 45, from Chaulnes to Vermand.
Pont Ges Brie	2·20	3·30	Arch (1 span)	Masonry	Road No. 85, from Villers-Carbonnel to Vermand.
,,	7	4	Wood (2 span)	Masonry abutments.	Road No. 85, from Villers-Carbonnel to Vermand. Over mill race.
,,	7	4·60	,, (2 ,,)	Masonry abutments and pier.	Road No. 85.

37

Location					
Pont les Brie	...	3	3·45	,, (1 ,,) ...	Masonry abutments.	,, ,,
,,	...	4	3·50	,, (1 ,,) ...	Masonry abutments.	,, ,, Locks underneath Bridge.
Over canal	...	14·60	3·70	Wood (1 ,,) ...	Swing bridge, between abutments 6·65	Road No. 201, from Amiens to St. Quentin.
Peronne, over river	...	10	5·85	Girder (2 span) ...	Masonry abutments and pier.	Route Nationale No. 17, Paris—Lille.
,,	...	5·50	5·90	,, (1 ,,) ...	Masonry abutments.	Route Nationale No. 17, Paris—Lille.
,,	...	3·90	10·30	,, (,,) ...	Masonry abutments.	Route Nationale No. 17, Paris—Lille.
,,	...	9·05	3·80	Drawbridge (2 span) ...	One iron girder 5½ metres and drawbridge.	Route Nationale No. 17, Paris—Lille.
,,	...	10·60	8·90	Arch (2 span) ...	Masonry ...	Route Nationale No. 17, over mill race.
Over canal	...	6·80	3·80	Drawbridge (1 span) ...	Masonry abutments.	Route Nationale No. 17.
Clery, over river	...	8·40	3·85	Wood (3 span) ...	Piles ...	Clery—Omiecourt Road.
,,	...	11·95	3·10	,, (2 ,,) ...	Masonry pier and abutments.	,, ,,
,,	...	4·10	1·65	,, (1 ,,) ...	Piles ...	,, ,,
,,	...	7·10	1·55	,, (2 ,,) ...	Masonry pier and abutments.	,, ,,
,,	...	11·50	3·70	,, (3 ,,) ...	Masonry abutments and piles, two mine chambers.	Omiecourt—Flaucourt Road, No. 6.
,,	...	10	4·30	,, (3 ,,) ...	Masonry abutments and piles.	Omiecourt—Flaucourt Road, No. 6.
,,	...	6	4·70	,, (1 ,,) ...	—	Omiecourt—Flaucourt Road, No. 6.
Feuilleres, over river	...	13·40	3·40	,, (2 ,,) ...	—	Feuilleres — Combles Road (146).
,, ,,	...	6	3·40	,, (1 ,,) ...	—	Feuilleres — Combles Road (146)

APPENDIX C—continued.

BRIDGES OVER THE SOMME AND SOMME CANAL—continued.

Town.	Length, metres.	Breadth, metres.	Type.		Remarks.
Feuilleres, over river	6·60	3·40	Wood (1 span)	...	Feuilleres — Combles Road (146).
"	5·20	3·40	" (2 ")	...	Feuilleres — Combles Road (146).
Over canal	14·60	3·60	Swing (1 span)	...	Feuilleres — Combles Road (146). Between abutments 6·65 metres.
Blaches, over canal	17·20	3	Wood (1 ")	...	To farm of Bazincourt.

BRIDGES OVER THE RIVER GERMAINE.

Douilly	4	6	Arch (3)	...	Masonry ...	Douilly—Villers—St. Christophe Road.
"	2	6	Wood	...	—	Ham—Margerie Road (Ch. vicinal).
Sancourt	5·20	8·95	Girder	...	Masonry abutments.	Chateau—Thierry—Bethune Road (Route Nle.).
Offoy	4·30	2·50	Wood (Footbridge)	...	—	Offoy—Viefville footpath.

BRIDGES OVER THE OMIGNON RIVER.

Pocuilly	4	4	Wood	...	Masonry abutments.	Country road.
Tertry	5·40	3·70	Culvert	...	One arch ...	Road, for Tertry.
"	11·60	7·0	Wood	...	Masonry abutments.	Road No. 202, from Peronne to St. Quentin.

Monchy Lagache	...	11·50	7·25	Arch...	Road No. 34, from Nesle to Rolsel.
,, ,,	...	4·50	3·35	Wood	Country road.
Devise	...	5·95	8·20	Culvert	Road No. 45, from Chaulnes to Vermand.
,,	...	10·20	8·20	Wood	Road No. 45, from Chaulnes to Vermand.
,,	...	5·50	3	Arch...	Country road, from Devise to Mons-en-Chaussee.
Athies	...	11·20	10	Arch...	Route Nationale No. 37, Chateau Thierry—Bethune.
,,	...	5·90	10·35	Culvert	Route Nationale No. 37, Chateau Thierry—Bethune.
,,	...	14·40	5·40	Arch...	Road No. 103, from Ennemain to Mons-en-Chaussee.
Pontru	...	2	9	,,	Road No. 10.
Maissemy	...	3	5	,,	Country road.
Vermand	...	4	7·30	,,	Road No. 4, Tertry to St. Quentin.
,,	...	4	4·50	,,	Road No. 88, Rolsel to Roupy.
Marteville	...	2·90	—	,,	Road.
Caulaincourt	...	3·40	4	,,	Road No. 13, from Caulaincourt to St. Simon.

BRIDGES OVER THE COLOGNE RIVER.

Tincourt Boucly	...	6·45	8	Girder	Masonry abutments	Road No. 88, from St. Christ.
Cartigny	...	6·45	3·90	Wood	,, ,,	Road No. 199, from Peronne.
Doingt	...	4·85	4	,,	Country road.
,,	...	7	6·60	Arch	Span, 4·40 metres; masonry	Route Nationale No. 37, Chateau Thierry—Bethune.
Flamicourt	...	6	8	Girder	Masonry abutments	Road No. 199, from Peronne.

APPENDIX C—*continued.*

BRIDGES OVER THE TORTILLE RIVER.

Town.	Length, metres.	Breadth, metres.	Type.		Remarks.
Etricourt—Manancourt	6·15	3·55	Arch	Span, 4·15 metres	Road No. 72, from Rolsel.
Moislains	5·75	4·35	,,	,, 4·40 ,,	Road No. 43, from Peronne.
Allaines	5·80	4·64	,,	,, 3·60 ,,	From Allaines to Clery.
,,	7·70	4·64	Girder	Masonry abutments.	Ordinary road.
,,	4·65	6·20	Arch	Masonry	Route Nationale, No. 37, from Chateau Thierry.
,,	8·90	3·90	Wood	Masonry abutments.	Country road.
Halle	10	7·20	Culvert	Masonry	Road No. 213, from Doullens.

APPENDIX C—*continued*.

LIST OF BRIDGES OVER CANAL DU NORD.

No. and Locality.	Road on which Situated.	Description of Bridge.	Span.	Width of Road-way.	Remarks.
			Metres.	Metres.	
1. Arleux	Country road	Fixed iron girder	32·00	3·00	
2. Palluel	Arleux-Epinoy	,,	30·00	5·00	
3. Bcourt St. Quentin	Ecourt St. Quentin-Oisy le Verger	,,	32·00	3·00	
4. Sauchy-Cauchy	Lagnicourt-Brunemont	,,	30·00	5·00	
6. Marquion	Arras-Cambrai	,,	32·00	5·50	
7. Sains-les-Marquion	Baralle-Bourlous	,,	32·00	5·00	
8. Inchy-en-Artois	Queant – Sains-les-Marquions.	,,	32·71	5·00	Under construction. Girders in position; roadway not completed. Temporary bridge alongside.
9. Inchy-en-Artois	Chemin Vicinal Moeuvres–Sains-les-Marquions.	,,	30·00	3·00	
10. Moeuvres	Moeuvres-Bourlon	,,	32·70	3·00	
11. Moeuvres	Moeuvres-Graincourt	,,	30·00	3·00	
12. Moeuvres	Bapaume-Cambrai	Fixed straight span Skew span	30·00 30·37	5·50 —	Skew, 81 deg.
13. Graincourt	Graincourt-Demicourt	Fixed iron girder	30·70	3·00	
14. Flesquières	Flesquières-Demicourt	,,	32·00	3·00	
15. Havrincourt	Havrincourt-Demicourt	,,	30·70	3·00	
16. Havrincourt	Havrincourt – Hermies. Also Railway, Bapaume-Cambrai.	Masonry arch	38·70	11·00	Roadway, 6·50 m.
17. Hermies	Chemin Vicinal Hermies-Metz-en-Couture.	Fixed iron girder	30·00	3·00	

Appendix C—continued.

List of Bridges over Canal Du Nord—continued.

No. and Locality.	Road on which Situated.	Description of Bridge.	Span.	Width of Roadway.	Remarks.
			Metres.	Metres.	
18. Hermies	Chemin Vicinal Hermies Ruyalcourt	Fixed iron girder	30·00	3·00	
19. Hermies	Chemin Rurale des Processions	,,	32·00	3·00	
20. Ruyalcourt	Hermes-Ruyalcourt	Masonry arch	30·00	5·00	
22. Etricourt	Rocquigny - Equancourt	Masonry skew arch— Straight span	32·00	5·00	Skew 80 deg.
		Skew span	32·49	—	
23. Etricourt	Etricourt—Equancourt	Masonry arch	30·00	3·20	
24. Etricourt	Chemin Vicinal Etricourt—Nurlu	Fixed iron	30·00	3·20	
25. Manancourt	Manancourt—Nurlu	,,	30·00	5·00	
26. Moislains	Country road	,,	32·00	3·20	
27. Moislains	Moislains—Nurlu	,,	30·00	3·20	Under construction. Girders in place and ramps built, but not metalled. Roadway incomplete.
28. Moislains	Moislains—Templeux	,,	30·00	5·00	Under construction. Traffic maintained by the old bridge.
29. Moislains	Moislains—Allaines	,,	32·00	5·00	Under construction.
30. Allaines	Allaines—Bouchavesnes	,,	32·00	3·20	Under construction.
31. Allaines	Allaines—Cléry	,,	32·00	3·20	Skew 80 degrees.
32. Feuillaucourt	Avesnes—Peronne	Masonry skew Straight span	—	5·50	Under construction.
		Skew span	30·00	—	
			30·46		

APPENDIX D.

DISTANCE MEASURED FROM :—
    ATHIES—MT. ST. QUENTIN (PERONNE).

BAPAUME—ARRAS ROAD TO ST. QUENTIN—CAMBRAI ROAD.

No. 1 Road (14 miles)—

Peronne-Roisel	7 miles.
Roissel-Bellicourt	7 ,,

No. 2 Road (18½ miles)—

Brioche-Nurlu	6½ miles.
Nurlu-Ronssoy	7 ,,
Ronssoy-Le Catelet	5 ,,

No. 3 Road (18½ miles)—

Beaulencourt-Fins	8½ miles.
Fins-Gouzeaucourt	4 ,,
Gouzeaucourt-Bois Mailland	6 ,,

No. 4 Road (18½ miles)—

Bapaume-Bertincourt	6½ miles.
Bertincourt-Gouzeaucourt	8½ ,,
Gouzeaucourt-Bois Lateau	3½ ,,

No. 5 Road (19½ miles)—

Sapignies-Havrincourt	12 miles.
Havrincourt-Marcoing	4½ ,,
Marcoing-Rumilly	3 ,,

No. 6 Road (18½ miles)—

Ervillers-Vaux	4 miles.
Vaux-Boursies	6 ,,
Boursies-Cambrai	8½ ,,

APPENDIX E.

Town.	Identification on squared map, 1/40,000.	Length, metres.	Breadth, metres.	Type.	Remarks.
RAILWAY BRIDGES OVER THE RIVER SCARPE (CANALISED).					
Fampoux ...	51b. II. 24a	16·30	—	Brick (3 arches)	Height above water, 6 m. Paris—Lille Railway.
RAILWAY BRIDGES OVER LA SENSEE CANAL.					
Aubigny-au-Bac ...	(51b.) R. 15b.	—	12	Girder ...	Masonry abutments. Cambrai—Douai Railway.
RAILWAY BRIDGES OVER LE COJEUL RIVER.					
Boisleux-au-mont ...	(51b.) S. 9d.	25·50	5	—	Masonry. Nord Railway.
" ...	(51b.) S. 11c.	11	5	—	" Boisleux—Marquion Railway.

RAILWAY BRIDGES OVER LA SENSÉE RIVER.

Town.					
Croisilles	...	(51b,) T. 29a.	...	...	13·50	6	—	Masonry	...	Boisleux — Marquion Railway.

RAILWAY BRIDGES OVER THE RIVER ESCAUT (CANALISED).

Town.	Length, Metres.	Breadth, Metres.	Type.	Remarks.
Cambrai	...	3	—	Steel	—	Cambrai-Douai Railway.

RAILWAY BRIDGES OVER THE ST. QUENTIN CANAL.

| Marcoing ... | ... | 15 | 5·26 | Girder ... | Masonry abutments, towpath, 4. | Cambrai—St. Just Railway. |
| St. Quentin ... | ... | 23·95 | 7·04 | ,, ... | Footpath. | Velu—St. Quentin Railway. |

APPENDIX E.—*continued.*

Town.	Length, Metres.	Breadth, Metres.	Type.		Remarks.

RAILWAY BRIDGES OVER THE SOMME CANAL.

Town.	Length, Metres.	Breadth, Metres.	Type.		Remarks.
Offoy	25	4·20	Girder	Masonry abutments (mine chamber)	Albert—Ham Railway.
Peronne, over river...	20	5·60	"	Masonry abutments (mine chamber)	St. Just—Cambrai Railway.
Peronne, over canal...	33	5·60	"	Masonry abutments (mine chamber)	St. Just—Cambrai Railway.

RAILWAY BRIDGES OVER LA TORTILLE RIVER.

Town.	Length, Metres.	Breadth, Metres.	Type.		Remarks.
Halle	4	4·20	Girder	Masonry abutments	Albert—Ham Railway.

RAILWAY BRIDGES OVER THE COLOGNE RIVER.

Town.	Length, Metres.	Breadth, Metres.	Type.		Remarks.
Doingt	5	4·20	Girder	Masonry abutments	Albert—Ham Railway.

RAILWAY BRIDGES OVER THE OMIGNON RIVER.

Athies	...	5	4·20	Girder	...	Masonry abutments.	Albert—Ham Railway.
Vermand	...	4	—	Arch	...	Masonry	Velu—St. Quentin Railway (no parapets).

RAILWAY BRIDGES OVER THE CANAL DU NORD.

15.	Marquion	...	45	Single Line. 11	Skew girder, 32 degrees. Arch ...	—	Marquion—Cambrai Line.
16.	Havrincourt	...	38·70	...	...	Masonry, railway, 4·50.	Bapaume—Cambria Line—(also Havrincourt—Hermies Road).
21.	Le Chelle	...	45	Single Line.	Fixed iron girder, skew bridge.	—	Velu—St. Quentin Line.
33.	Halle	...	—	—	—	Not yet started	Doullens—Peronne Line.
34.	Halle	...	—	—	—	,,	Albert—Hain Line.

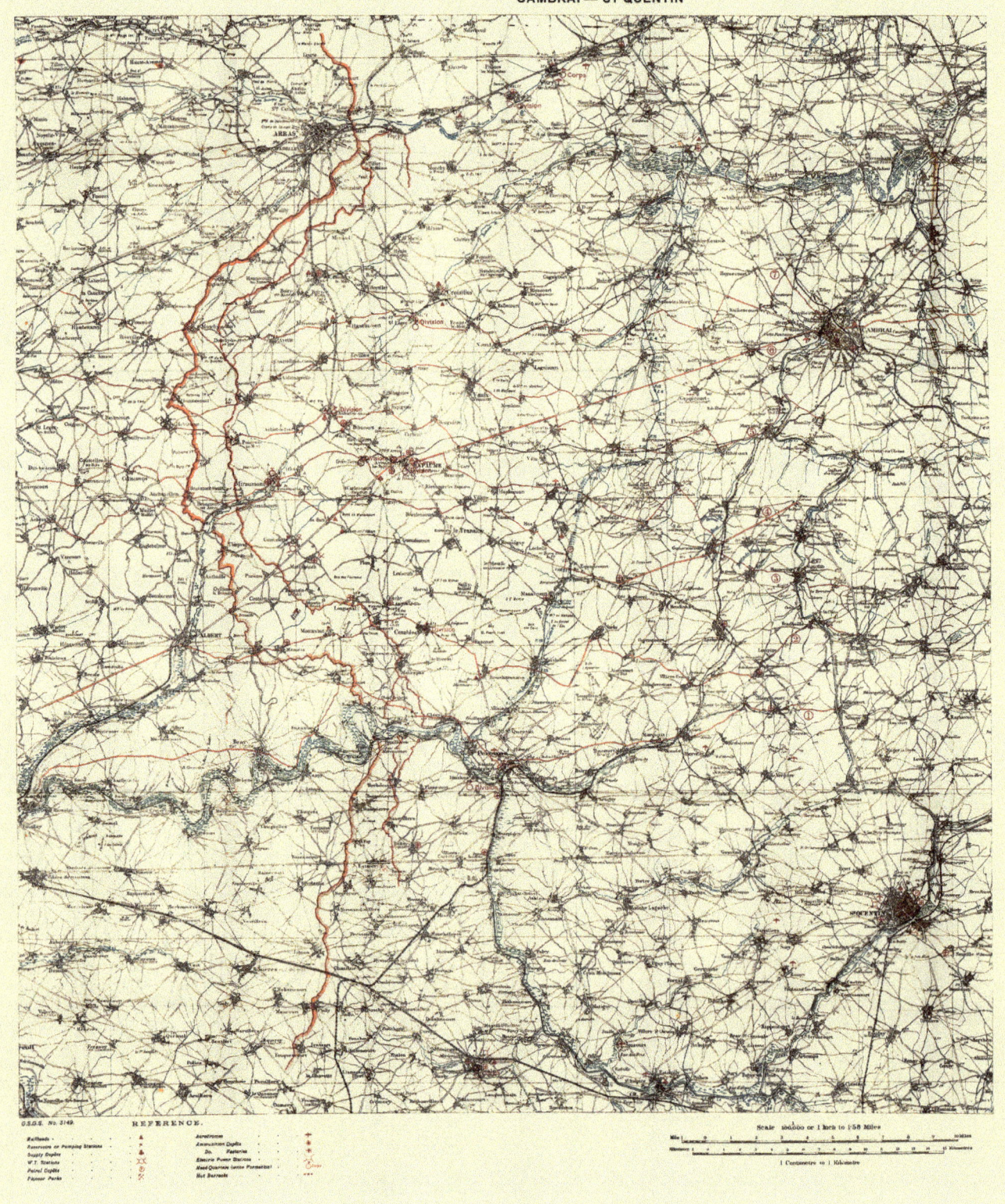

CAMBRAI — St QUENTIN

**MAP
CAMBRAI - St QUENTIN
spread 1**

**MAP
CAMBRAI - St QUENTIN
spread 2**

Spread 1

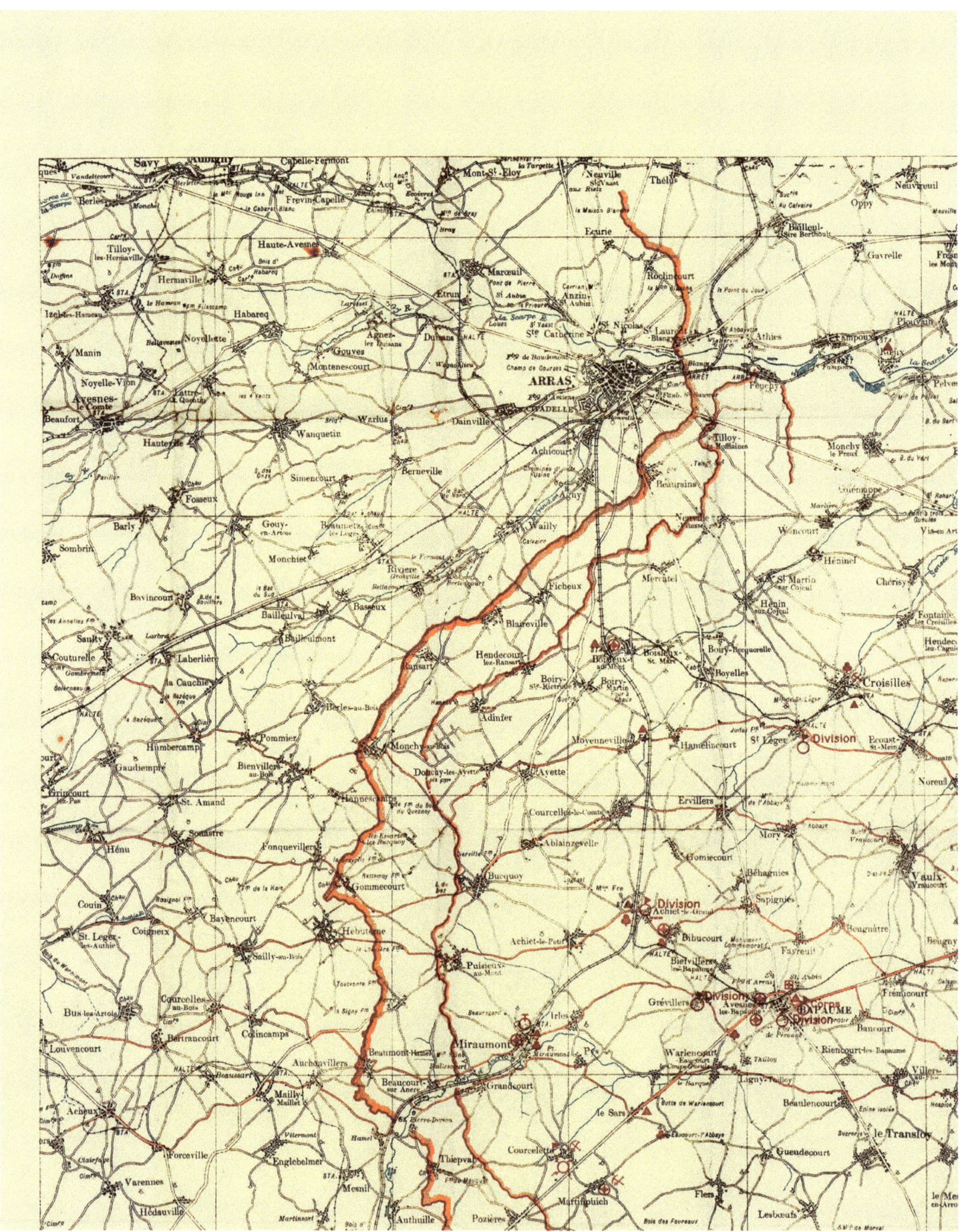

CAMBRAI — St QUENTIN

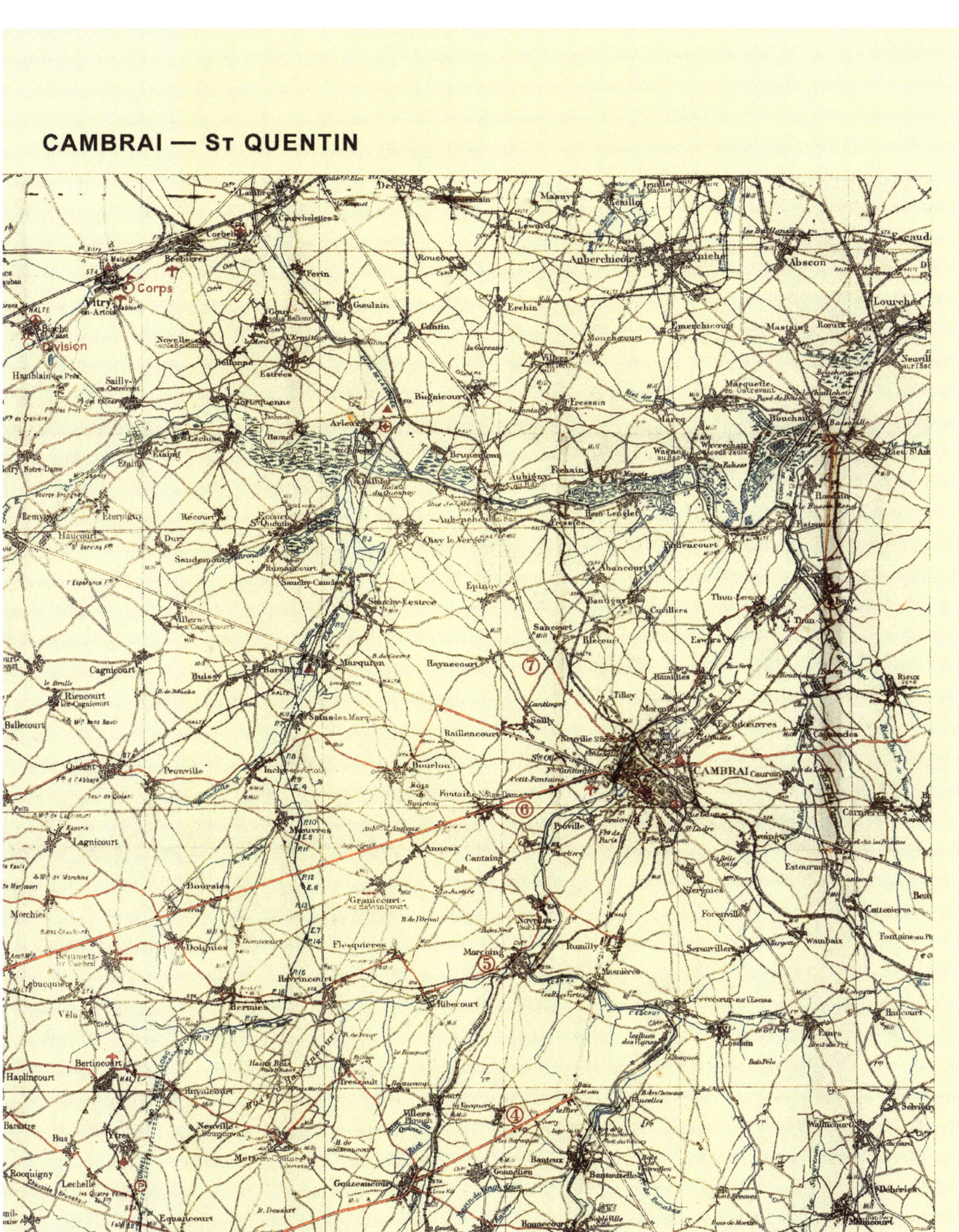

Spread 2

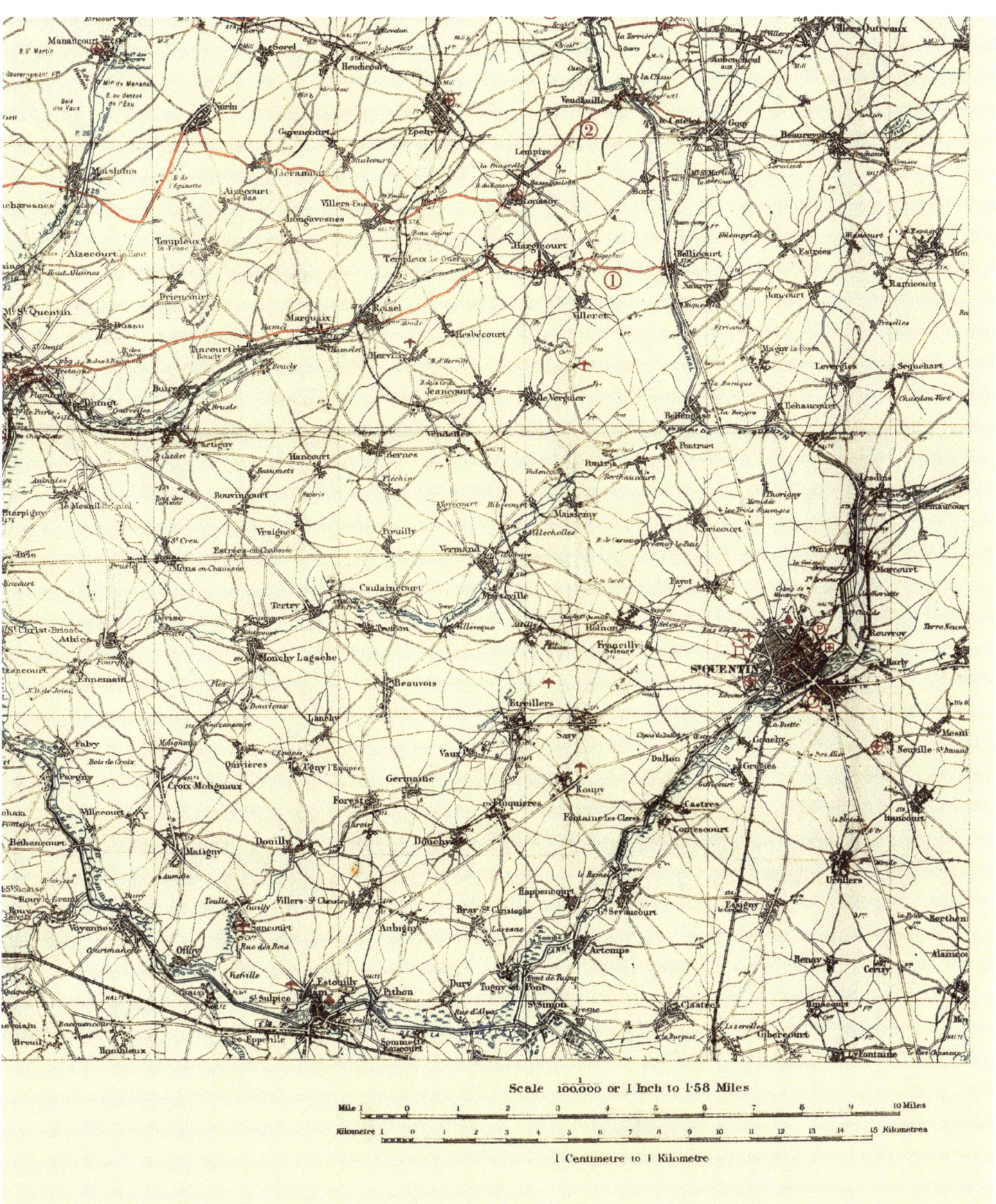

Scale 1/100,000 or 1 Inch to 1·58 Miles

1 Centimetre to 1 Kilometre

NAVAL & MILITARY PRESS
WWW.NAVAL-MILITARY-PRESS.COM

GUIDES TO THE ALLIED LINE AND MEMORIALS ON THE WESTERN FRONT

Works such as these N&MP productions formed the 'Roots of Remembrance' that 100+ years on still attract pilgrims in their droves to visit the Western front and its memorials to the fallen

THEY ARE ALWAYS IN PRINT AND ALWAYS AVAILABLE

Definitely books to add to your backpack when taking a pilgrimage to France, and have a seasoned veteran or expert vividly describe the action or memorial

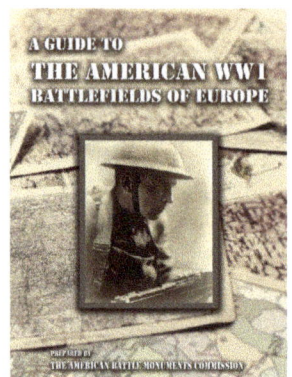

A GUIDE TO THE AMERICAN WW1 BATTLEFIELDS OF EUROPE
Prepared by the American Battle Monuments Commission

A solid reference for those who wish to know about the American evolvement in the Great War, and also good for family members discovering where a doughboy great-grandfather fought – this classic is a good place to start. This 1927 guide is organised by region and campaign: Aisne-Marne, St. Mihel, Meuse-Argonne, Champagne, and the areas north of Paris including Flanders, Ypres, the St. Quentin Canal Tunnel and Cantigny. It includes narrative, photographs and maps.

9781474540483

BRITISH MEMORIALS OF THE GREAT WAR

A historical and attractive guide to the various national, regimental and divisional memorials on the Western Front, with photographs and maps, and also notes on memorials further afield including Gallipoli. Published in the 1930s by pioneer travel agency and printing company Dean & Dawson, who conducted battlefield visits. An interesting contemporary tour prospectus is reprinted with this book that outlines the various tours to the Somme, Ypres, Arras etc, along with the maps that accompanied the original publication.

9781474537995

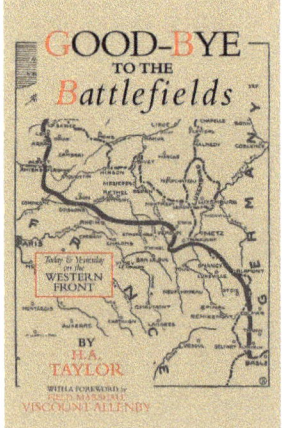

GOOD-BYE TO THE BATTLEFIELDS
Today and Yesterday on the Western Front

Captain Taylor walks the battlefields of the Western Front 'as they are today (1928)', with good descriptions of the battlefields, relics and memorials during the inter-war period, along with 1920s photographs of towns and villages, cemeteries, memorials and battlefield areas during the period of post-war reconstruction.

With his reminiscences of events, that lend a real atmosphere, his memory and feet "follow our khaki-clad columns moving northward". This is definitely one book to add to your backpack when taking a pilgrimage to France.

9781474536967

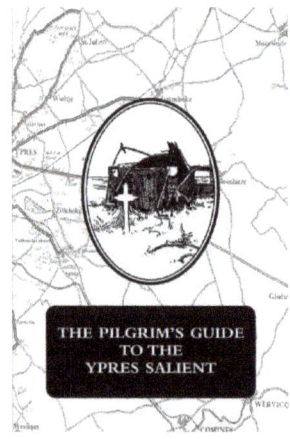

PILGRIM'S GUIDE TO THE YPRES SALIENT

One of the earliest guidebooks to the Ypres Salient, stated by the author to be compiled for the ex-servicemen who may wish to visit the graves and battlefields of the Great War. Unusually, and interestingly, it includes essays on various aspects of service in the Salient: Hugh Pollard on infantry, Walter Gardiner on mining, F. Worthington on RAMC Work; Machine Guns in the Salient by 'Maxim', etc.

9781474536738

TWENTY YEARS AFTER - THE BATTLEFIELDS OF 1914-1918 THEN & NOW THREE VOLUME SET

'Twenty Years After – The Battlefields of 1914-1918 Then & Now' is not a publishing curiosity but a fascinating piece of Great War history that is still of much value today.

Alongside the atmospheric images is an extensive text, describing many operations and locations on all Fronts, but mainly France & Flanders. With its thousands of superb photographs, this is a fine reference work that was originally issued in many parts but now much more convenient in this bound form.

9781783315505

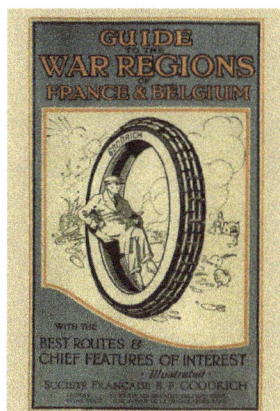

GUIDE TO THE WAR REGIONS OF FRANCE AND BELGIUM
With the Best Routes & Chief Features of Interest

Published in the 1920s by Goodrich tyre company, 'Guide to the War Regions of France & Belgium' was aimed at the relatively new phenomenon and the independent motorist. Packed with useful information including coloured maps, photographs, together with advice for motorists and details of seventeen different war regions, each with map, route, hotels, historical and economic accounts, a short history of the operations and war facts. These war regions include: The Marne, Champagne, Verdun, Nancy, Vosges, Alsace, Lorraine, Ardennes, Belgium, Yser, Artois, Picardy, Chemin-des-Dames, Somme, Cambrai, Arras and Ypres. Unlike our reprint of 'The White Cross Touring Atlas of the Western Battlefields' that is concerned with visiting the war graves of the fallen, this guide is angled towards the battlefield tourist.

9781783319473

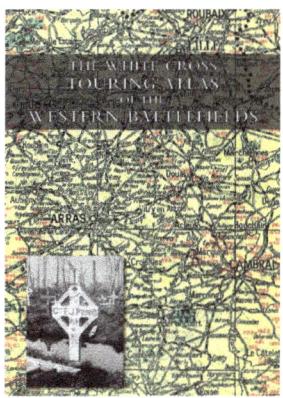

THE WHITE CROSS TOURING ATLAS OF THE WESTERN BATTLEFIELDS

An early historical Great War battlefield guide the whole Western Front, complete with 64 good colour maps, a descriptive text and a War Graves Index of over 1700 cemeteries. The main value to this book, that is now very scarce in it's original printing, is that it shows the locations of many of the British cemeteries that were later consolidated by the CWG.

9781783315758

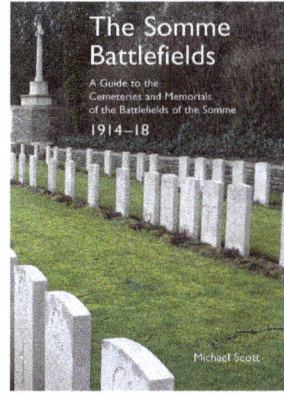

SOMME BATTLEFIELDS
A Guide to the Cemeteries and Memorials of the Battlefields of the Somme 1914-18

An introduction to the battlefields of the Somme through the cemeteries and the memorials. Every cemetery within which is buried a man recorded by the CWGC is covered. The story of the cemetery, the local memorials and information of the lives and war experiences of some of those buried in each cemetery is told.

9781783312900

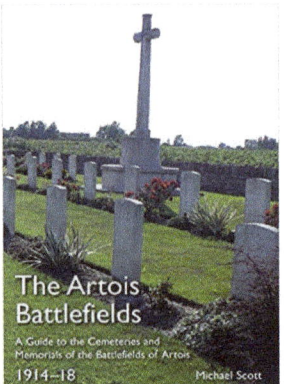

ARTOIS BATTLEFIELDS
A Guide to the Cemeteries and Memorials
of the Battlefields of Artois 1914–18

This introduction to the battlefields of Artois is told through the war cemeteries and those buried within. The story of the cemetery, local memorials and lives and war experiences of some of those buried in each cemetery are covered.
9781783314768

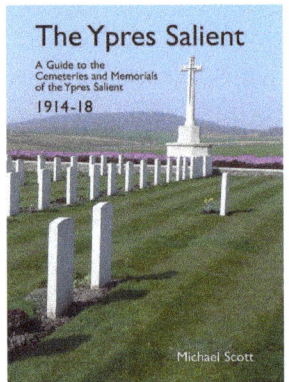

YPRES SALIENT
A Guide to the Cemeteries and Memorials
of the Ypres Salient 1914-18

An exciting new version of an earlier work, this introduction to the battlefields of the Ypres Salient is through the cemeteries and those buried within. The story of the cemetery, local memorials and lives and war experiences of some of those buried in each cemetery is told.
9781783313518

SILENT CITIES
An illustrated guide to the war Cemeteries & Memorials
to the missing in France & Flanders 1914-1918

The classic guide to the War Cemeteries in France and Flanders. A work of enduring appeal to the battlefield tourist.
9781843422624

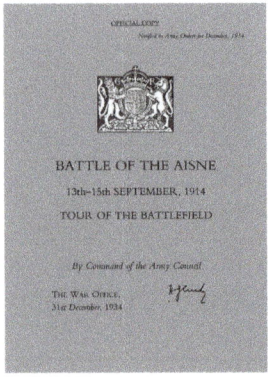

BATTLE OF THE AISNE
13TH-15TH SEPTEMBER 1914,
TOUR OF THE BATTLEFIELD

Official War Office guide to the First Battle of the Aisne in September 1914 in which the BEF helped the French push the Germans across the River Aisne. The battle marked the change in the Great War between the war of movement and trench warfare.
9781845740351

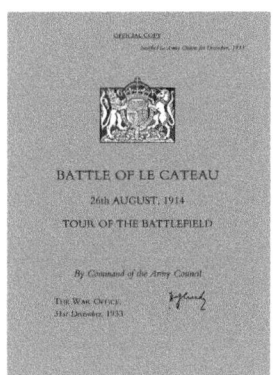

BATTLE OF LE CATEAU 26TH AUGUST 1914, TOUR OF THE BATTLEFIELD

Combined War Office map package and tour guide to Le Cateau, where the BEF stood and halted the German juggernaut for a day on August 25th 1914.

9781845740337

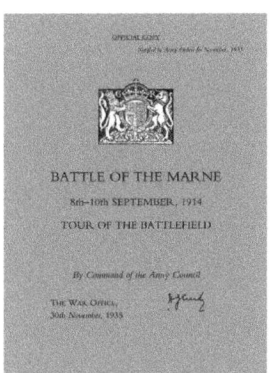

BATTLE OF THE MARNE 8TH-10TH SEPTEMBER 1914, TOUR OF THE BATTLEFIELD

The 3-day Battle of the Marne in September 1914 was the turning point of the Great War. The German capture of Paris was thwarted by the action of the French armies and the BEF. This is the official War Office guide to the battle and the battlefield.

9781845740344

YPRES: THE HOLY GROUND OF BRITISH ARMS

An important early Great War guidebook, written by a man who played a critical role in the Ypres we see today. Henry Beckles Willson was a fierce opponent of the rebuilding of Ypres, feeling that the horrific losses sustained there by the British Army.

9781783317530

naval-military-press.com

www.ingramcontent.com/pod-product-compliance
Lightning Source LLC
Chambersburg PA
CBHW041700090426
42743CB00024B/3490